THEN & NOW

BOSTON'S SOUTH END

Hundreds of members of the Harvard University Student Regiment march west in uniform precision along Columbus Avenue in the South End during a Preparedness Parade held in Boston on May 27, 1916. Columbus Avenue, named after the Italian explorer Christopher Columbus (1451–1506), was laid out in 1868 and formed an axis stretching from Park Square to the Roxbury line. It is still one of the major thoroughfares in the South End. (Author's collection.)

Then & Now
BOSTON'S SOUTH END

Anthony Mitchell Sammarco
Contemporary Photographs by James Z. Kyprianos

Published by Arcadia Publishing
Charleston SC, Chicago IL, Portsmouth NH, San Francisco CA

Printed in Great Britain

Library of Congress Catalog Card Number: 2005934211

For all general information contact Arcadia Publishing at:
Telephone 843-853-2070
Fax 843-853-0044
E-mail sales@arcadiapublishing.com
For customer service and orders:
Toll-Free 1-888-313-2665

Visit us on the internet at http://www.arcadiapublishing.com

*In honor of Richard O. Card, founder and
first president of the South End Historical Society.*

Three uniformed maids pose for a photographer in the late 19th century in Boston's South End. The red-brick bowfront façade row houses share common architectural details, building materials, uniform setback, and dormered mansard roofs. These planned streetscapes created an urbane, unified, and desirable neighborhood in the mid-19th century. (Author's collection.)

CONTENTS

Roman Catholics, bearing blessed palms, leave the front doors of the Cathedral of the Holy Cross in Boston's South End after high mass on Palm Sunday in 1930. The massive lancet arched doorway, paired entrances, and walls hewn of granite and Roxbury pudding stone added to the overall impressiveness of Patrick C. Keeley's Gothic design. (Courtesy of the Boston Public Library, Print Collection.)

INTRODUCTION

With its distinctive red-brick row houses, lush green parks, upscale restaurants, the new Boston Center for the Arts and controversial metallic façade, and many other welcoming amenities, Boston's South End has become not just a popular place to reside but also a destination.

The present South End (not to be confused with the Colonial South End of Boston) was originally a narrow land mass surrounded by tidal flats. It connected the mainland, starting at Roxbury, to the town of Boston. In the early 19th century, Charles Bulfinch devised a plan to lay out a grid pattern of streets and parks. Within this plan he designed the twin-oval Columbia Square, which is now known as the Blackstone and Franklin Squares. Known as the Neck (present day Washington Street), it would be filled in the 1840s by the South Cove Company in order to create a level land mass of 70 new acres. This land was laid out with streets for Boston's burgeoning population, and many of these streets were named after cities and towns in the commonwealth.

By the 1850s, the filling of the South Cove and the South Bay created the present-day South End. In the mid-19th century, the South End had become one of the more desirable places to live in the city, and affluent merchants and businessmen moved to the area. It was an oasis of new urbanity with wide tree-lined streets, gas streetlights, and brick paved sidewalks. There were many squares and parks; among them the Rutland, Worcester and Chester Squares, Concord Square, and Union Park. The streetscapes of uniform red-brick row houses shared repetitive bowfronts, uniform setback and height, and the newly fashionable mansard roofs. This style was popularized by noted Boston architect Nathaniel J. Bradlee (1829–1888), and it attracted many who built or bought new houses on speculation. According to an 1872 edition of *Boston Illustrated*, the "South End of Boston . . . is a district of residences."

Major thoroughfares in this area—Washington, Tremont, and Albany Streets and Shawmut, Columbus, and Harrison Avenues—crossed the South End and connected old Boston with the new land west of Massachusetts Avenue. The South End was virtually completed by 1870, but by that time the newly created Back Bay of Boston attracted people who desired the social cachet of this new area, and thereafter the South End steadily lost favor. The lands on the southern periphery were developed by placing Gridley J. Fox Bryant's Boston City Hospital on the south side along Harrison Avenue, then known as Front Street. Boston College was located across the street, next to the Immaculate Conception Church. Numerous places of worship swiftly followed their parishioners to the new neighborhood. The Cathedral of the Holy Cross was envisioned by Patrick J. Keeley as a soaring twin-towered pudding stone church, but was unfortunately scaled down due to its immense weight on the filled land. Following the Panic of 1873, the once desirable neighborhood that had shown such promise for two decades quickly gave way to an influx of working class citizens. By 1900, the South End had become a neighborhood with a diverse population of working class residents, and new immigrants arrived every day. The South End became so diverse that in 1891 the first settlement house in Boston, the South End House, was established. It served the needs of these immigrants in ways ranging from teaching English as a second language to Americanization programs, clubs, and activities. The once fashionable row houses were subdivided into lodging houses and apartments and thereby changed the character of the South End immeasurably. The Boston Elevated Railway Company built the El, an elevated train, along Washington Street. It ran day and night and caused noise and blight that remained unabated for seven decades.

By the early decades of the 20th century, the South End had become a "vibrant, economically poor but culturally rich, dynamic community" of American society. Jews, Syrians, Greeks, Italians, Portuguese, Chinese, West Indians, and African Americans lived in the area. In 1922, *Boston, A Guide Book* wrote that the "South End is now a faded quarter," surprisingly less than seven decades after it began with such aplomb and hopeful anticipation. Following World War II, the city of Boston began a series of urban renewal projects that addressed decades of housing neglect. Among these projects were the Castle Square and the Cathedral Veterans Housing Projects, which demolished entire blocks of 19th-century housing in order to make way for new multi-family housing. With these new affordable housing developments in the South End, the one square mile neighborhood began to attract new residents. Many came to appreciate the impressive 19th-century architecture and squares laid out a century earlier, but they also saw a need for more housing. In the 1970s, increasing Puerto Rican and Dominican immigration created an even more diverse South End. The Inquilino Boricuas en Acion (Puerto Rican Tenants in Action) took over Parcel 19 in 1976 and built Villa Victoria, an Hispanic tenant-run housing project designed by John Sharratt Associates. With young energetic professionals beginning a revitalization that continued from the 1970s onward, the South End quickly embraced a large and vibrant gay and lesbian community. This community still continues to add to the urbane upbeat character that makes the South End among the destinations of the city of Boston.

In 1973, Boston's South End was listed on the National Register of Historic Places as not only having the largest number of intact original Victorian row houses in the United States, but also because it is an important representation of a planned 19th-century development. A decade later, the 500 acre neighborhood was declared a Landmark District by the city of Boston, with the ultimate goal of preserving what remains after urban renewal destroyed entire areas five decades ago. It is now the largest preserved Victorian neighborhood in this country.

Worcester Square, seen here about 1875, looking towards Washington Street, displays the repetitive bowfront red-brick town houses that flourished in the South End from the 1850s onward. Here, four-story row houses share uniform setback, roof height, mansard roofs with dormers, and a high flight of stairs. The park had a central fountain with a double alley of trees on either side of a central pathway. (Courtesy Boston Public Library, Print Collection.)

Chapter 1
THE EARLY
SOUTH END

Looking north on the Neck (present day Washington Street) in this 1815 watercolor, it is obvious that there were few houses along this narrow strip of land. This area had fewer than two dozen houses between Lenox Street and Columbia Square in the early 19th century. As a horse-drawn carriage approaches Concord Street the barrenness of the land is evident, though the dome of the Massachusetts State House could be seen on the upper left. (Courtesy Boston Athenaeum.)

A trio of Federal houses once stood on the Neck, present day Washington Street, near the current site of the Cathedral of the Holy Cross. On the far left is the home of Thomas and Mary Barnard Blake, in the center is the home of Daniel Weld, and in the foreground one can see the home of John and Hannah Weld Williams. These red-brick Federal houses dated between 1793 and 1810 and represented the new South End's penchant for impressive residences. (Author's collection.)

The Lancaster House, at the corner of Washington and East Concord Streets, was a three-story center entrance Federal house. Here it is seen on the far left, adjacent to the South Burial Ground. Described as "half road house, half tavern" it was a popular stop along the Neck for weary and thirsty travelers. On the far right can be seen the multi-layered cupola of Boston College on Harrison Avenue. Today, an attractive apartment building occupies the site. (Courtesy Historic New England.)

The Deacon House, built in 1848 on Washington Street, was designed by Jean Lemoulnier and Gridley J. Fox Bryant. The front faced West Concord Street and boasted a high brick wall, double gates, and a center porter's lodge. It was the home of Edward Preble and Sarah Annabella Parker Deacon, and it started a fashionable trend as the first French-style brick house in Boston with a mansard roof and porte cochere. The house was sold at an auction in 1871, and the Massachusetts Normal Art School occupied the former mansion, after which it was drastically remodeled in the late 19th century as Deacon Halls, a popular dance hall. On the left was the

Commonwealth Hotel. Today, a large apartment block occupies a part of the site. (Courtesy Boston Museum of Fine Arts.)

Union Park, originally known as Weston Street, was laid out in the mid-1840s with four-story red-brick row houses. It created an impressive backdrop to the square. Seen here in an 1885 photograph, 40 through 46 Union Park show the ideal South End row house. Cast iron railings lead up to front doors with rococo detailed lintels, heavy cornices, and dormers project from roofs and cupolas. Union Park attracted notable and socially prominent residents, among them Gov. Alexander Hamilton Rice, the Walter Baker chocolate heiress Eleanor Baker, S. S. Pierce, and Dr. George Gilbert Smith. (Courtesy Richard O. Card.)

In this 1860 view, Chester Square has an enormous three-level white-painted cast iron fountain with a cast iron fence encircling it. It is in the center of the largest of the South End squares. Elegant, well designed, and imminently respectable, the two center cupolaed houses at 546 and 544 Massachusetts Avenue were those of the Crowell and Howes families. Their front doors opened to face the central fountain in the square. Massachusetts Avenue was put through the center of the square in the mid-1950s, and its four-lane street ruined the placidity and refinement achieved a century earlier. (Courtesy David R. Hocker.)

Looking along Warren Avenue from Columbus Avenue in 1875, the Church of the Disciples can be seen on the right at West Brookline Street. The spire of the Warren Avenue Baptist Church is visible on West Canton Street. On the left, the spire of the Berkeley Temple can be seen at Berkeley Street. Today, a park is in the center and named for Harriet Tubman (1820–1913), the "black Moses" who conducted 300 slaves to the north prior to emancipation in 1863. There is a life-sized bronze statue of the former slave, sculpted by Fern Cunningham, in the park. Columbus Square faces the landscaped park. (Courtesy Massachusetts Historical Society.)

orcester Street, looking south from Tremont Street in 1875, shows the uniform streetscape created by the South End row houses, and a corner of the Tremont Street Methodist Church is visible on the left. One of the more famous residents of this street was Hezekiah Butterworth of number 28. Author of *Zigzag Journeys*, he was also on the staff of the *Youth's Companion* for many years, located in the South End's Pledge of Allegiance Building. Today, the row house on the right corner has been remodeled with the Tremont Market on the first floor, and Worcester Street is heavily leafed with mature trees. (Courtesy private collection.)

At the corner of Washington Street and Chester Square (now Massachusetts Avenue) were two impressive row houses with corner quoining, oriel windows, and fashionable mansard roofs. They represent the epitome of mid-19th-century urban design. These two houses were at 1747 and 1745 Washington Street, the site of Olympia Flower Shop and now a Dunkin Donuts in the rear, and on the far right can be seen the Smith Block (now Minot Hall) on Washington Street. (Courtesy Boston Public Library, Print Collection.)

Waltham Street, which extends from Tremont Street to Harrison Avenue, is one of the ladder streets of the South End. By the time of the Civil War, it was built up with row houses of various designs, from flat façades to the more prevalent bowfronted façades. From the left, 96, 98, and 100 Waltham Street were single-family row houses, but today are apartments and condominiums. (Courtesy Boston Public Library, Print Collection.)

This row of five high-stooped South End row houses is at the corner of Dartmouth Street and Columbus Avenue, and was proposed by Nathaniel J. Bradlee as the prototype for the South End—solid and dignified. The former row houses had a two-story brick addition added after the staircases were removed for commercial purposes, and on the corner is Clery's restaurant. (Courtesy Boston Public Library, Print Collection.)

Tremont Street, between Rutland and West Concord Streets, had a row of eight houses referred to as Poet's Row, for each house had a wood bust of a different poet above the portico. Seen in a *c.* 1870 photograph, 694 to 708 Tremont Street creates an impressive streetscape. It was probably designed by Nathaniel J. Bradlee and built in 1858. Today, only the left three, (694, 696, and 698) survive. The Boston Fire Department was built on the right. (Courtesy Boston Athenaeum.)

Looking north on Columbus Avenue from Rutland Square in 1880, the elegant streetscape of row houses is punctuated on the left by Alexander R. Estey's Union Congregational Church. On the right is the spire of the Second Universalist Church, built in 1872 at the corner of Clarendon Street. In the center can be seen the tower of the Boston & Providence Depot at Park Square. The tower of the I. M. Pei designed Hancock Tower and the Art Deco Cram & Ferguson designed Hancock Building can be seen in the distance of the now photograph. (Courtesy Richard O. Card.)

This is an 1868 view of Columbus Avenue, looking east from Massachusetts Avenue, starting from Park Square and ending at the Roxbury line. The avenue had row houses built in the 1865–1875 period. They were converted into lodging houses and apartments after the Panic of 1873, when many houses were repossessed by banks and sold at drastically reduced rates. The spire of the Union Congregational Church (now the Union Methodist Church) and the two towers of the John Hancock Mutual Life Insurance Company can be seen in the distance. (Courtesy Historic New England.)

In this *c.* 1875 photograph, the corner of Washington and West Canton Streets has impressive row houses, but a fancy dry goods store has opened on the first floor of 1045 Washington Street. This indicates the changing economy of the South End and the encroachment of commercialism into the once strictly residential neighborhoods. Today, the entire block has been razed and is used as a parking lot. (Courtesy Boston Public Library, Print Collection.)

Worcester Square, looking towards Boston City Hospital's administration building on Harrison Avenue, was laid out in 1852 to create a mirror image of bowfronted row houses undulating around a central green space. The park, seen in this *c.* 1870 photograph, has been enclosed by a black cast iron fence, and young trees line the center path and fountain. Notice the gas lanterns projecting over the dirt paved street and the uniformity of the row houses in height, setback, and building material. (Courtesy Historic New England.)

Chapter 2
THE SQUARES

Blackstone Square was laid out by Charles Bulfinch in the early 19th century. Here, in a photograph taken around 1865, the large black cast iron fountain is encircled by a granite-rimmed pool, with two parasol-shaded ladies enjoying the bucolic scenery. The prominent spire of the Shawmut Congregational Church can be seen in the center. It was designed in the Romanesque style by John D. Towle and built in 1852 on Shawmut Avenue, between West Canton and West Brookline Streets. This church was later used as the Armenian Holy Trinity Church and then Iglesia de Dios. (Courtesy David R. Hocker.)

In this *c.* 1859 photograph, a well-dressed woman holding a silk parasol relaxes in Chester Square, with three young girls behind her. In the rear is a small red-brick chapel that was used by the Springfield Congregational Society, until their church was built in 1860. Notice the young trees and the lavishly planted garden, all enclosed by a black cast iron fence. This scene was a major attraction in the new South End. Today, Massachusetts Avenue cuts through the square, which is illuminated at night by lollipop-domed streetlights. (Courtesy David R. Hocker.)

Chester Square was laid out in 1850 by Ezra Lincoln and was the epitome of the grand South End Squares, connecting Shawmut Avenue and Tremont Street. The center of the square had a three-story white-painted cast iron fountain with a large granite-curbed fish pond. It is said to have been "much frequented by the pretty children and trim nursery-maids of the neighborhood." The immaculately swept pathways were shaded by trees and gardens. They were planted to be enjoyed by residents, some of whom can be seen in the distance. Today, a four lane highway cuts through the center of the once bucolic park. (Courtesy David R. Hocker.)

Designed by Ellis Chesbrough and William Parrott, the center of Union Park in the 19th century had a white-painted iron fountain, lavishly planted gardens, arbors, and espaliered vines and shrubs. A massive spar of white-painted pine stood in the center, from which Old Glory flapped in the wind. The columned belfry of the South Congregational Church, designed by Nathaniel J. Bradlee and built in 1862 at 15 Union Park Street, can be seen in the distance. In 1887, Temple Ohabei Shalom purchased this building and worshiped here until 1925, when it was sold to the Greek Orthodox Church of Saint John the Baptist. Today, the heavily leafed square is one of the most attractive places of residence in Boston. (Author's collection.)

Union Park, seen in 1916 looking
towards Shawmut Avenue, has
mature shade trees lining the center
path in the fenced enclosure. The
center fountain and the pine spar can
be seen through the leafy enclosure,
and an electric streetlight can be
seen to the right of the center gates.
Laid out in the 1850s, the cache of
Union Park would be retained with
impressive row houses occupied by
prominent residents. Notice the wood
blinds on the windows and the lack of
automobiles. (Courtesy James Roche.)

Worcester Square was laid out in 1852. It has a large center oval park with a two-tiered white-painted center fountain, enclosed by a black cast iron fence. Photographed around 1870, the row houses on the left face west and many of the windows sport striped canvas awnings, though it is obviously late spring. The impressive domed administration building of Boston City Hospital at Harrison Avenue acts as a visual axis for the square. Bryant's design enhances the planned symmetry of the streetscape. Today, Hite Radio & TV Shop anchors the square at the corner of Washington Street. (Author's collection.)

Blackstone Square, one of the two squares created by Charles Bulfinch known as Columbia Square, was named for the Reverend William Blackstone. Blackstone was the first English settler in Boston and his house stood on the western slope of Trimount, now Beacon Street. This edge of the 2.3 acre square had large row houses and small wood-framed buildings, including the Chin You Chinese Laundry. These buildings were demolished in 1922 in order to make way for the John J. Williams Municipal Building at the corner of Shawmut Avenue and West Brookline Street. After 1875, much of the South End's high expectations had changed and infill housing, often of inferior quality, was built in the area. (Courtesy Boston Public Library, Print Collection.)

The Smith Block is an Italianate commercial block located on Washington Street at the corner of West Springfield Street. Dry goods stores, such as George Moir Provisions and William Anderson and Company, are located on the first floor and shaded by awnings. The Hotel Olympia apartments are above, and Minot Hall is on the third floor. In front of the block is a horse-drawn delivery wagon of the Kennedy Butter and Egg Company, a grocery purveyor that was well-known a century ago. (Courtesy Historic New England.)

Chapter 3
ALONG THE NECK

Williams Market was designed by noted Boston architect Gridley J. Fox Bryant and opened in 1855 at the corner of Washington and Dover (now East Berkeley) Streets. Stalls offered fresh meats, poultry, and fish on the first floor and a meeting hall was above. On the right are 1144 and 1148 Washington Street two bowfronted row houses that still survive with the Eagle Stables on the far right. On the far left is a row of flat fronted row houses on Dover Street, a portion of which still survives. The market was later used as the vaudeville Grand Theater and Museum, and later was the site of Harry the Greek's, a popular workman's clothing store. (Courtesy Boston Athenaeum.)

By 1899, 1583 to 1569 Washington Street (on the left at the corner of Rutland Street) had dry and fancy goods stores installed on the first floor of the row houses, which drastically changed the character of the block. Today, the site is used as a community garden. (Courtesy Historic New England.)

By 1899, the southwest corner of Washington and Rutland Streets had row houses that were transformed with a tobacconist, confectionary shop, lunch-room, laundry, and apothecary. Today, an attractive residential block has been built on the site. (Courtesy Historic New England.)

The St. James Hotel, seen on the far left, was an elegant five-story hotel on East Newton Street, facing Franklin Square. In this pre-1914 image, it is being used as the Franklin Square House, a residence for working women. Later, an addition was added that replaced the early brick Greek Revival house on the corner. Today, the former hotel, in addition to its 20th-century addition, has been converted to senior citizen apartments. It once served as the hospital exterior in the television drama *St. Elsewhere.* (Courtesy Richard O. Card.)

The Aaron Hill Allen House was designed by John McNutt and built in 1859 at the corner of Washington Street and Worcester Square. It is a large freestanding brownstone house with Flemish gables, pedimented lintels, oriels, heavy corner quoining, and a dormered mansard roof capped by a four-sided cupola, and is the epitome of a mid-19th-century residence. Allen leased the house to the Central Club in 1871 when he moved to the more fashionable Back Bay. After his death it was sold to the Catholic Union of Boston, then used by Boston College High School, and then the Lebanese American Club. The Allen House has recently been converted to condominiums. (Courtesy Richard O. Card.)

This block on Washington Street, between Dover (now East Berkeley) and Decatur Streets, was a bustling commercial area in 1899. The Madison Block was a four-story multi-dormered building with an advertisement for Madison Pants painted on its end wall. The block must have been teeming with daily activity, as the area held a coffee house, a Chinese laundry, a tailor, and a shoeshine and hat cleaning shop. The block has changed beyond recognition with modern buildings. (Courtesy Historic New England.)

The Salvation Army People's Palace was on Washington Street, adjacent to Franklin Square. The tracks of the Boston Elevated Railway (the El) can be seen on the left, and on the right a portion of the Cathedral of the Holy Cross is visible. The building was demolished in 1948 for the creation in 1950 of the Cathedral Veterans Housing Project, a federally subsidized undertaking designed by Harold Field Kellogg. (Courtesy South End Library.)

The Union Congregational Church was designed by Alexander R. Estey in an English Gothic style. It was built between 1870 and 1875 on Columbus Avenue between West Rutland and West Newton Streets. The congregation moved from Essex Street to the new South End in 1870, but the impressive tower and spire of Roxbury pudding stone was not completed until five years later. The Union Methodist Church, formerly known as the Fourth Methodist Episcopal Church, worships here today. (Author's collection.)

Chapter 4

PLACES OF WORSHIP

The Springfield Street Congregational Church was designed by Nathaniel J. Bradlee and built in 1860 at 157 West Springfield Street. It was a prominent classically inspired church made of red brick and limestone. Its façade had flat Doric pilasters supporting a simple cornice and center pediment, with doorways surrounded by prominent keystone quoining. Later it was the home of the Third Presbyterian Church, and the Ebenezer Baptist Church worships here today. (Courtesy Boston Athenaeum.)

The Church of the Unity was designed by Thomas Silloway and is said to have been "simple and tasteful in architecture," even at the time of its erection. Built in 1859 on West Newton Street, between Tremont Street and Shawmut Avenue, the impressive colonnaded façade has six Corinthian columns supporting a massive pediment. The church was prosperous, financially as well as religiously. Demolished in 1898, the Zion Evangelical Lutheran Church was built on its site, and later All Saints Lutheran Church worshiped here. It was converted in 1986 to the Jorge Hernandez Cultural Center. (Courtesy David R. Hocker.)

The Tremont Street Methodist Episcopal Church was designed by J. H. Hammatt Billings and built in 1862 at the corner of West Concord and Tremont Streets. Designed as a plain Gothic Style church, and perhaps the first church in Boston built of Roxbury pudding stone, the two towers and their spires add greatly to the overall design and prominence of the streetscape. Today, the New Hope Baptist Church worships here. (Courtesy David R. Hocker.)

The Berkeley Temple Congregational Church, built in 1862, is at the corner of Berkeley Street and Warren Avenue. The Odd Fellows hall is on the left and in the center distance the spire of the Central Congregational Church is visible. It is now the Church of the Covenant in Boston's Back Bay. Today, the Calderwood Pavilion at the Boston Center for the Arts and the Atalier, a fashionable condominium development, are on the left. The church was replaced with a police station and is now being tastefully converted into condominiums. (Courtesy Massachusetts Historical Society.)

The New South Free Church held a Unitarian society that was originally at the "church green," Summer and Bedford Streets, in the old South End of Boston. The structure was built at the corner of Tremont and Camden Streets. Today, this is the People's Baptist Church. In 1898, it became St. Paul's church, an African American church. A two-story community center was added along the Washington Street side of the church. (Courtesy Milton Public Library.)

The Shawmut Congregational
Church was designed by C. E.
Parker and built in 1864 at the corner
of West Brookline and Tremont
Streets, with a seating capacity of
1,500 worshipers. It had an impressive
design with a square Lombardy
bell tower containing a four-sided
clock visible from both directions
on Tremont Street. There was a
disastrous fire in the 1970s and it
was then converted into affordable
housing. Taino Tower was created
using a shortened tower and portions
of the church. It was reconstructed by
Communitas, Inc. in 1991.

The Church of the Immaculate Conception was designed by Patrick C. Keeley (1816–1896) and dedicated in 1861 at the corner of Harrison Avenue and East Concord Street. It was built of hammered New Hampshire granite, without tower or spire, and a statue of the Virgin Mary is within the façade pediment. A statue of the Savior with outstretched arms surmounts the church. Still under the auspices of the Jesuits, the Arthur Gilman interior was drastically renovated in the 1980s in order to create the Jesuit Urban Center. It was designated a Boston Landmark in 1987. (Author's collection.)

The Cathedral of the Holy Cross was designed by Patrick C. Keeley and built between 1866 and 1875 on Washington Street between Union Park and Malden Streets. It is an impressive early English Gothic church built of Roxbury pudding stone as well as granite and limestone trimmings. The 330-foot Great Tower was never completed, however, due to its immense weight. Although never completed, the cathedral is still the largest in New England. On the right is Ellis & Kerr with a three bay engine house. Today it is the site of the South End Boys Club. (Author's collection.)

The Second Universalist Church was built in 1872 at the corner of Columbus Avenue and Clarendon Street. It was built of Roxbury pudding stone with a soaring bell tower and a polychromatic slate roof. It is said to have been "exceedingly cheerful and pleasant with painted windows." A large multi-storied condominium was built in 1990 on this site and it is now known as 75 Clarendon Street. (Courtesy Richard O. Card.)

The Warren Avenue Baptist Church, originally the old Baldwin Place Church in the North End, was built in 1866 at the corner of West Canton Street and Warren Avenue. In the 20th century, it was used successively as the Seventh Day Adventist Church and the Church of Our Lady of the Annunciation—a Syrian Roman Catholic church. The church was demolished in 1968, and the site is today the James Hayes Park. (Courtesy David R. Hocker.)

The Church of the Disciples was built in 1869 at the corner of West Brookline Street and Warren Avenue. It was a prominent city church, a free church, and a social church. The members as well as the pastor took part in the operations of the church. After 1904, the First United Presbyterian Church (formerly located on Berkeley and Chandler Streets) worshipped here. Today, the Concord Baptist Church worships at this site. In this *c.* 1870 image 195 and 193 West Brookline Street can be seen on the far right. They are in the process of being built. (Courtesy David R. Hocker.)

The Franklin Union Building was built in 1908 at the corner of Berkeley and Appleton Streets and "dedicated to opportunity" for both men and women in the field of trades. Named for Boston born Benjamin Franklin (1706–1790), this was the new trade school for Boston. It was funded by Franklin as well as by Andrew Carnegie, who matched the sum to "afford to young men who are working at a trade an opportunity to increase their knowledge and proficiency." (Author's collection.)

Chapter 5

SCHOOLS

The Franklin School was built for girls in 1852 and was located on Ringgold Street between Waltham and Hanson Streets. It was a four-story red-brick school and was dedicated to Boston native, Benjamin Franklin (1706–1791). He was born on Milk Street and later moved in diplomatic circles, becoming Ambassador to France. Franklin is referred to as the father of electricity and his likeness adorns American 100 dollar bills. Today, Ringgold Park is on the site of the school. (Courtesy Boston Athenaeum.)

Girls' High School was built between 1869 and 1870 on West Newton Street. It was a red-brick school with a granite basement, sandstone window and door lintels, and a massive cupola. On the far left the colonnade of the Church of the Unity can be seen and on the right, 67 and 65 West Newton Street are visible. These row houses were designed and owned by Nathaniel J. Bradlee, who speculated on real estate as well as designing architecture. The O'Day Playground occupies the site of the school today. The All Saints' Lutheran Church, a German Gothic style church built in 1899, is on the far left (now the Jorge Hernandez Center), and an apartment block on the right. (Courtesy Richard O. Card.)

The Rice School (later known as the Rice-Bancroft School) was designed by William Ralph Emerson and Carl Fehmer. It was built in 1868 on Dartmouth Street between Warren Avenue and Appleton Street. The school was named for Alexander Hamilton Rice (1818–1895), a former mayor of Boston, United States congressman, governor of Massachusetts, and a resident of Union Park in the South End. The structure was converted into condominiums in 1985 by Arrowstreet, Inc., minus the imposing mansard roofs on each corner tower. (Courtesy Richard O. Card.)

The impressive Boston Latin and English High School was designed by the first Boston city architect, George A. Clough (1843–1914). It opened in 1877 and combined the two most prominent high schools in the city during the 19th century. Purportedly the largest public school in the world at the time, the dual façades were 420 feet in length and were bound by Warren Avenue and Dartmouth and Montgomery Streets. The school was demolished in 1949. Today, the McKinley Elementary and Technical High Schools (formerly the Charles Mackey Middle School) are on the site. They were built in 1959 and designed be Thomas F. McDonough. (Courtesy William Dillon.)

Boston College was designed by Louis Weissbein and built adjacent to the Church of the Immaculate Conception on Harrison Avenue. Founded in 1860, and conducted by the Fathers of the Society of Jesuits, it was important in that it offered a collegiate education to the sons of the aspiring Roman Catholic immigrants. The college was an impressive our-story red-brick building with a hip roof surmounted by a belfry. After 1913, when the college moved to Chestnut Hill, it was used as the Boston College High School. It was later converted into the church rectory. (Courtesy William Dillon.)

The rusticated double doors of the city of Boston Fire Headquarters entered into a large space where chemical engines were kept, waiting to be drawn by swift horses to the scene of a fire. It was designed by Boston city architect Edmund March Wheelwright (1854–1912) in the last decade of the 19th century. The yellow-brick and limestone stringcourse design gave a sophisticated detail to the building. Today, this is the Pine Street Inn, a refuge for Boston's homeless. (Author's collection.)

Chapter 6

INSTITUTIONS

The Odd Fellows Hall was built in 1872 at the corner of Tremont, Berkeley, and Warren Streets. It was an imposing white granite five-story Gothic Revival building with lancet doorways, windows, and dormers and a mansard roof surmounted by a clock. The Willcox and Gibbs Sewing Machine Company occupied the first floor. The Odd Fellows (IOOF), a fraternal and social organization that stressed friendship, love, and truth, had a large hall on the fourth floor. Today the Atalier, an imposing condominium building, and the Calderwood Pavilion of the Boston Center for the Performing Arts are located on the site. (Courtesy David R. Hocker.)

The Parker Memorial Hall, named in memory of noted theologian Rev. Theodore Parker (1810–1860), was built in 1873 at the corner of Berkeley and Appleton Streets by the 28th Congregational (Unitarian) Society. Later used as a social and community center, it was subsequently known as the Caledonian Building and then as the Magna Building, as the Magna Film Company was located here. It was eventually the site of the groovy Boston Tea Party, a popular dance nightclub. The club was gutted by fire in 1972 and rebuilt in 1975 by the Boston Architectural Team. Today, there is a 7-Eleven store on the first floor and numerous apartments above. (Courtesy David R. Hocker.)

The Washington Market was built in 1870 at the corner of Washington and Lenox Streets. One of many stalled markets in the city, it was described as being 250 feet long and contained 100 stalls for shoppers. The stalls were described as being "clean and bright as well as roomy." Today, the site has modern buildings and a waiting station for buses. (Courtesy David R. Hocker.)

The St. James Hotel was a 400 room Second French Empire structure designed by John R. Hall, and its impressive façade faced Franklin Square. It was built in 1868 by proprietor Maturin Murray Ballou, who owned *Ballou's Pictorial Drawing Room Companion*. It was made of brick with granite facings, and a center pavilion was surmounted by a domed roof. The flanking corner towers had heavily quoined corners and a mansard roof. The hotel was later used as the New England Conservatory of Music and is today senior citizens apartments. To the left on East Newton Street, fine Italianate row houses built in the late 1850s are being replaced by a newer and larger building. (Courtesy David R. Hocker.)

The New England Conservatory of Music (formerly the St. James Hotel) fronted onto Franklin Square at East Newton Street. It was used as a school from 1882 until 1902, and then it moved to the Fenway. The building was an impressive Second French Empire design that was converted from a luxury hotel into classrooms, office space, and a woman's dormitory. In the 20th century, the building was used as the Franklin Square House, a working women's residence. It was converted into senior citizen apartments in 1976 by the Boston Architectural Team and Archplan, and now it overlooks a park of mature trees. (Courtesy William Dillon.)

The Commonwealth Hotel was built in 1869 as an impressive residential hotel on Washington Street, between Worcester and Springfield Streets. Built in the Second French Empire style, its façade was covered in white marble and was described as being "of a most handsome and ornamental style of architecture." Later known as the Langham Hotel and then the Hotel Washington, it was finally demolished, and now a nondescript apartment block is on the site. (Author's collection.)

The Berwick Hotel was built in 1878 at the corner of Columbus Avenue and Holyoke Street. It was a Ruskinian Gothic design with a multi-bayed polychromatic façade, stringcourse bands, and decorative iron railings. It was one of many fashionable residential hotels being built in the South End and Back Bay neighborhoods during this time. It was later known as Dr. Flower's Hotel and then the Hotel Plaza, and the once popular German restaurant, Heidelberger Rathskellar, was on the lower level. Today, a parking lot occupies the site. (Courtesy Boston Public Library, Print Collection.)

The Cyclorama was designed by Cummings & Sears and built in 1884 on Tremont Street. It was built to display the massive *Battle of Gettysburg,* a full color rendition by Paul Philippoteaux of the Civil War battle. The 360 degree painting circled the interior walls of the red-brick and crenellated building. Later used as an automobile station for two decades, and then as the Boston Commercial Flower Exchange, it was also the site of shows that needed the cavernous hall. In 1970, the structure became the Boston Center for the Arts. Today, the crenellated towers poke above the remodeled façade as the Hancock Tower looms above. (Courtesy Richard O. Card.)

The Columbia Theater was located between 978 and 986 Washington Street. Built in 1827 as the South Congregational Church, it was converted into an elaborate Moorish Revival theater in 1891, long after the congregation had built a new church and moved to Union Park Street in 1861. It was a popular place with legitimate theater, vaudeville acts, silent films, and talkies, but it was demolished in 1957 when it could no longer compete with larger and more opulent venues around the city. Today, the Teradyne parking garage is on the site, with their South End headquarters adjacent to it. (Courtesy William Dillon.)

The Castle Square Theater and Hotel was built in 1894 at the corner of Tremont and Chandler Streets, now the site of the Animal Rescue League. It housed a theater in which light and standard operatic companies performed, with store fronts on the ground floor and a hotel above. The theater was renamed the Arlington Theater following World War I and was razed in 1932. (Courtesy Boston Public Library, Print Collection.)

The National Theater was designed by Clarence H. Blackall and built in 1911 on Tremont Street, between the Cyclorama (left) and the Hotel Clarendon (right). Advertised as the largest Theater in Boston, it had 3,500 seats priced at a nickel or a dime. Today, the Calderwood Pavilion at the Boston Center for the Arts is on the site, with the Atalier above. (Courtesy Richard O. Card.)

The city of Boston Fire Headquarters was between Bristol Street (now Paul Sullivan Way) and Dover (now East Berkeley) Street. Designed by Boston Architect Edmund March Wheelwright and built in 1894, the yellow-brick crenellated tower emulated that of the Palazzo Vecchio in Florence, Italy. The building was also used for many years as a fireman's training school and men would climb the sides of the tower to improve their rescue skills. The structure was converted into the Pine Street Inn in 1980 by Childs, Bertram, Tsekares, and Casendino, offering shelter to the city's homeless. (Courtesy William Dillon.)

This image shows Boston Firehouse 72 (Engine No. 22, Ladder 13), located at 72 Warren Avenue. Designed by Dorchester architect John A. Fox (1835–1920), it is a classical revival two-bay firehouse with Doric pilasters supporting a lintel and corner quoining. The roof pergola was a unique and attractive feature, with pleasant views of the neighborhood. Later used as the South End office of the Boston Redevelopment Authority, it is now condominiums. (Courtesy private collection.)

Looking towards Park Square along Columbus Avenue, the tower of the Boston & Providence Railroad depot, designed by Peabody & Stearns, can be seen in the center distance. On the left is the People's Temple, which was a Methodist church. On the right, the battlement tower of the First Corps Cadets Armory at Arlington Street is visible. This block of Columbus Avenue has given way to commercialism, with large businesses, first floor shops, and apartments above. (Author's collection.)

Chapter 7
BUSINESS OVERLAY

The corner of Washington Street and Massachusetts Avenue (on the left) was a grand entrance to Chester Park, as the avenue was originally known, that led to the palatial Chester Square. The two row houses (1747 and 1745 Washington Street) were built as single family houses, but by 1899 they had shops on the first floor and apartments above. Between these row houses and the Smith Block (now Minot Hall) on the right, was the small wood-framed house of W. H. Wardwell, a local photographer. The building on the corner is now vacant, though it once housed an attractive apartment building and the famous Olympia Flower Shop. (Courtesy Historic New England.)

This 1895 image shows the junction of Columbus Avenue and Chandler and Dartmouth Streets. It displays how streetscapes were originally planned in the mid-19th century with uniformly designed bowfronted row houses, but the façades changed due to commercial intrusion. On the right is an apothecary, complete with a mortar and pestle sign, showing how homes often converted into first floor shops. Today, a small triangular shaped tree-shaded park is at this intersection, where the curved house once stood. (Author's collection.)

The elegance of Worcester Square was marred when an addition for three small shops was added to the rear of 1672 Washington Street. In this 1890 photograph, a clerk stands in the doorway of a grocery shop adjacent to a laundry shop and tailoring shop. The mature trees lining the path in the center park add a gracefulness to the rigid streetscape of the row houses. Today, they still create an impressive vista looking towards Boston City Hospital. (Courtesy Boston Public Library, Print Collection.)

Conklin's Corner was at the corner of Columbus Avenue and Dartmouth Street in a large four-story mansard roofed row house. Seen in 1900, the two-story establishment is complete with awnings shading the apartments above. In *The City Wilderness* Robert A. Woods writes, "A very large traffic rumbles through its streets without having any relation to it . . . people on its sidewalks have neither business duties nor home responsibilities within its borders." Today, Clery's restaurant is located here, with I. M. Pei's Hancock Tower looming above. (Author's collection.)

Cor. Mass. and Colum. Av's. Boston Mass.   506

A five-story apartment building was constructed at the corner of Massachusetts and Columbus Avenues in the late 19th century, with commercial space on the first floor and apartments above. The replacement or modification of earlier row houses began as early as the 1880s, in order to make better use of the space. The drug store and taxi cab stand adjacent to the Wellington Café, seen on the far right, opened in 1901. Philos & Kluris served fine food daily from 6 a.m. until midnight. Music played in the evenings and Sunday afternoons. (Courtesy James Roche.)

The Supreme Council of the Royal Arcanum was founded in 1877 at the South End home of Darius Wilson. The headquarters was built at 407 Shawmut Avenue at the corner of West Brookline Street in an impressive five-story hammered granite and red-brick building. The group was founded by immigrants seeking fraternal benefits, social interaction, and protection from financial hardships. It is still active today and is general in membership. It seeks to unite men and women of all backgrounds, trades, religious, and political beliefs. The common bond of the Society requires that members believe in a Supreme Being. Today, the structure is the Salvation Army Harbor Light Center. (Courtesy Boston Public Library, Print Collection.)

The Chickering & Sons Piano Factory is an enormous red-brick five-story factory designed by Edwin Payson and built in 1853. It is located on Columbus Avenue between Northampton and Camden Streets, and occupies an entire city block. Established in 1823 by Jonas Chickering, it employed four hundred hands and could produce 4,000 square pianos annually. In 1972, the factory was renovated by the firm of Gelardin, Bruner, Cott, Inc. It was converted into artist studios and apartments, and renamed the Piano Craft Guild. (Courtesy Richard O. Card.)

The Hallet & Davis Piano Company was a five-story Second French Empire factory with a center mansard roofed tower, located on Harrison Avenue between Brookline and Canton Streets. Founded in 1839 by George Davis, it employed 250 hands and had the capacity to produce 2,500 instruments annually. The company patented a suspension agraffe bridge, which reinforced the rigid upright bearing of the piano, allowing for a finer tone. The factory was later used by the Star Paintbrush Company until it was demolished in 1969, and is today unfortunately a vacant lot. (Courtesy William Dillon.)

The Emerson Piano Company had a large seven-story panel-brick factory on Harrison Avenue between Waltham and Union Park Streets. The company was founded in 1849 by William P. Emerson. The factory was designed by Alonzo Drisko and built in 1891. By 1900 it produced 150 pianos a week, and continued until it closed in 1922. Today, the former piano factory is flanked by an attractive tree shaded park. (Courtesy William Dillon.)

The Boston Elevated Railway was one of the first elevated train lines in the country and was popularly known as the El. It was built between 1899 and 1901 and traveled from the Forest Hills Station in Jamaica Plain to Boston. It followed Washington Street, the old Neck of the South End, and terminated at Sullivan Square in Charlestown. Here, at the intersection of Washington Street and Massachusetts Avenue, the Orange Line train travels east towards its next stop, Dover Street Station. On the left can be seen the Smith Block, now called Minot Hall. (Courtesy Alison Barnet.)

Chapter 8

TRANSPORTATION

This view, taken around 1870, faces west on Tremont Street at Montgomery and Clarendon Streets. A horse-drawn streetcar of the Metropolitan Line can be seen in the foreground, with the spires of the Shawmut Congregational Church and the Tremont Street Methodist Episcopal Church on the left. In the center is the Alfred Newhall Pianoforte Manufactory. The fashionable St. Cloud Hotel is directly behind it. The St. Cloud was designed by Nathaniel J. Bradlee and built in 1870 as a fashionable French Academic style apartment building, and it was restored in 1987 by Arrowstreet, Inc. Today, the Calderwood Pavilion at the Boston Center for the Arts and the Atalier are on the right. (Courtesy Massachusetts Historical Society.)

Looking east on Tremont Street in 1907, a man signals an electric streetcar to stop near Berkeley Street. On the left is the former Cyclorama, used from 1899 to 1922 as an automobile station, and was the location where Albert Champion invented the Champion sparkplug. In 1923, the building was sold to the Boston Commercial Flower Exchange and used as such until 1970, when the Boston Center for the Arts leased the building. Today, the multi-balconied Atalier looms above the Cyclorama and the Boston Center for the Arts. (Courtesy Bradley Clarke.)

In this 1919 image, Tremont Street at the corner of Waltham Street is being excavated as an electric streetcar waits for the workmen to finish. On the left is the Cyclorama building, and the Waldorf Theater (formerly the National Theater) marquee can be seen in the distance. Today, only automobiles, buses, and various bikes traverse Tremont Street. The Cyclorama and the Boston Center for the Arts can be seen on the left. Notice how close downtown Boston is in relation to the South End, with high rise office buildings looming above the streetscape. (Courtesy Bradley Clarke.)

The National Theater on Tremont Street was billed as the largest theater in Boston with its 3,500 seats. Here on a busy Tremont Street, complete with electric streetcars and automobiles, the marquee advertises a cabaret night in addition to the featured films. The theater was demolished in 1996. Today, the Calderwood Pavilion at the Boston Center for the Arts and the Atalier occupy the site. (Courtesy Boston Public Library, Print Collection.)

The Northampton Street Station on the Boston Elevated Railway was designed by Alexander Wadsworth Longfellow (1854–1943). It was an island station platform with a well-designed waiting room overlooking Massachusetts Avenue. Begun in 1899 and opened in 1901, it served as an important station because Boston City Hospital was only a block away. Today, 19th-century row houses survive with the Hotel Alexandra, an apartment building on the right, at the corner of Washington Street and Massachusetts Avenue. (Courtesy Thomas F. Connolly Jr.)

The Dover Street Station on the Boston Elevated Railway was at Washington Street and Dover (now East Berkeley) Street and built between 1899 and 1901. The elevated station was accessible by twin copper-roofed iron staircases and the station itself was built of copper and wood paneling. There were casement windows and decorative pilasters and the word "Dover" made of pressed metal could be seen in the pediment parapet above. The El has been removed and now the commercial streetscape is open to light and air. (Courtesy Alison Barnet.)

Along Washington Street were numerous stores in the shadows of the Elevated Railway's tracks. Folsom's Market was near the corner of Washington and Lenox Streets and was advertised as "Boston's Busiest Food Store" in the 1960s. It provided parking in the rear for the ascendancy of the automobile. Today, a nondescript apartment building occupies the site. (Courtesy Alison Barnet.)

This *c.* 1900 view looks east on Harrison Avenue from Massachusetts Avenue. Worcester Square, the Church of the Immaculate Conception, and Boston College are on the left side of the street. Boston City Hospital buildings are on the right. The hospital was founded in 1855 for the city's respectable poor and laid out between 1861 and 1864. It was placed on a seven acre tract adjacent to an emerging neighborhood that had high hopes and aspirations. Dedicated in 1864, Boston City Hospital has served the city admirably ever since. (Courtesy Boston Medical Center.)

Chapter 9
BOSTON CITY HOSPITAL

Boston City Hospital's administration building was designed by Gridley J. Fox Bryant (1816–1899). It was placed on Harrison Avenue on an axis running to Worcester Square. The impressiveness of the design (the tall dome was based upon that of Les Invalides in Paris) and the symmetry of the four pavilions made the new hospital's campus attractive and efficient. The building was demolished in 1934, and a less architecturally prominent structure was built to replace it. (Courtesy David R. Hocker.)

The left pavilion of Boston City Hospital was one of four designed by Bryant to create a "U" shaped forecourt to the hospital. The dormered mansard roof emulated those on the row houses in nearby Worcester Square. These pavilions contained segregated wards for patients and were connected to the administration building by an open granite colonnade and an underground passage. Today, the pavilion is unused and a parking lot is located on the former lawns. (Courtesy David R. Hocker.)

The Nurse's Home at Boston City Hospital was designed by Edmund March Wheelwright and built in 1898 behind the administration building. Its tall dome can be seen on the right. This home provided accommodations in addition to the Linda Richards House that was built in 1885 at the corner of Harrison Avenue and East Springfield Street. Today, the busy emergency room entrance is located here. (Author's collection.)

The Boston City Hospital Ambulance Station was designed by Boston city architect Edmund March Wheelwright and built in 1898 on Albany Street. Along with numerous other buildings, it created a hospital campus that extended from Harrison Avenue to Albany Street. The Ambulance Station was equipped with a separate Flemish step-gabled stable, since ambulances were pulled by horses until the early 20th century. Today, modern offices loom over Massachusetts Avenue. (Author's collection.)

ACKNOWLEDGMENTS

I would like to thank the following for their assistance, either directly or indirectly, in the researching and writing of this book: Jim Kyprianos for his skillful and insightful "now" photographs; Alison Barnet; Stephen Beaudoin; the Boston Athenaeum, Sally Pierce; Boston Medical Center; Boston Public Library, Print Collection, Aaron Schmidt; Richard O. Card, South End historian and founder of the South End Historical Society; Regina K. Clifton; Thomas F. Connolly Jr.; Rupert A. M. Davis; Dexter; William Dillon; Olivia Grant Dybing; eBay; the late Rosamond Gifford; Edward W. Gordon; Helen Hannon; Pauline Chase-Harrell; Historic New England, Lorna Condon; David R. Hocker; Stephen Kharfen; Massachusetts Historical Society; Milton Public Library; Museum of Fine Arts, Boston; Ellen Ochs; Michael M. Parise; J. B. Price; James Roche; Anthony and Mary Mitchell Sammarco; South End Branch Library, Anne Smart; South End Photo Lab, Casi and Stephen Walker; Erin Stone, my editor; the Urban College of Boston; and the Victorian Society, New England Chapter.

The Zion Church was founded in 1834 at the old Franklin School, and the congregation dedicated this particular church in 1846 at the corner of Shawmut Avenue and Waltham Street. The members were Evangelical Lutherans and all German immigrants. They worshipped here until 1898 and then built a new church on West Newton Street. As the demographics in the South End changed in the 20th century, the former church was remodeled by the Sahara Syrian Restaurant, serving ethnic foods to the numerous Syrians in the neighborhood. Today, the former church-cum-restaurant is used for storage, awaiting its next transformation. (Photograph by James Z. Kyprianos.)